Foreword

The art of bowling b [illegible] h, when linked togeth [illegible] g, delivery technique. It [illegible] is, gripping the bowl, st [illegible] m and stepping out car [illegible] ry styles. **There is no one correct way of arriving at the point of release of the bowl, only different ways** and in any one club it is unusual to find two players with virtually identical deliveries.

A common denominator in the deliveries of successful bowlers however, is the fact that their action is smooth, flowing and consistent, and at the point of release every bowl is grounded without 'bump' or 'wobble' and with machine like precision.

This manual highlights the importance of the correct approach to the delivery action which is the foundation for the improvement and future success of your game. The question and answer section identifies common faults affecting consistency and gives advice on how to correct them. The shot selection section considers the variety of shots to be mastered in a simple, 'Read the Head' format.

Concentration, a positive mental attitude towards each shot and lots of **correct** practice are the ingredients which will improve your game and bring success. This manual is a first step towards that goal.

The advice given in this booklet applies to both men and women but for the sake of brevity, the male gender only has been used throughout.

Choice of Bowl

For anyone starting the game of bowls it is essential that the correct size of bowl is selected. The type of grip you adopt, flexibility and size of the fingers, moistness or dryness of the hand, ability to control the bowl in variable conditions, are all related factors which can determine the size of bowl you choose. **The general rule of thumb is to choose the largest bowl you can handle comfortably without stretching your hand.** If the bowl can be held upside down at arm's length for a period of 10-15 seconds without strain then this is an indication that the bowl is the correct size for your hand (photograph A1).

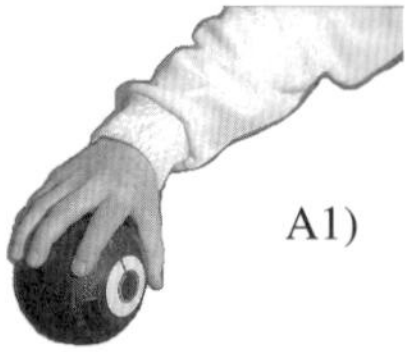

A1)

The weight of the bowl, whether it has grips or not, are other factors which have a bearing on bowl selection.

A heavy bowl is roughly equivalent in weight to a medium weighted bowl two sizes larger and so is more difficult to remove from the head (arguably, harder to promote **into** the head). They tend to be favoured by players with smaller hands. On damp, outdoor greens however, the heavyweight bowl can sink in to the grass making it more difficult to play to long jacks.

To have grips or not depends on your view as to whether they impede your hold on the bowl or assist it, especially in cold or wet conditions.

Finding the right bowl to suit can be a matter of trial and error. Ask the advice of your club coach and fellow members about why they chose their particular bowl and how their bowls perform on fast and heavy greens. If possible borrow various sizes and weights of bowl to try out before deciding to buy.

Grip

There are three main ways of gripping the bowl with variations of each:

The Cradle Grip (diagram B1)

The bowl is cradled in the palm of the hand with the fingers spread evenly around the running surface. The thumb is in a comfortable position at the side, on or below the centre disc.

Advantages

Most suitable for a medium/heavy green or where wet conditions may cause the bowl to slip in the hand. Less effort is required to propel the bowl a full length on heavy greens.

Disadvantages

The cradle grip does not use the sensitive parts of the fingers (fingertips) as the bowl rests in the palm of the hand. Consequently this grip is less appropriate for precise weight adjustments than either the claw or fingertip grips.

The Claw Grip (diagram B2)

The claw grip is somewhat similar to the cradle grip, except that the bowl sits further forward on the fingers with the thumb in a comfortable position above the centre disc, creating a gap between the palm of the hand and the bowl.

Advantages

An 'all round' grip for slow, medium and fast geens. The middle and third fingers are used for delicate weight adjustments as the bowl leaves the hand.

Disadvantages

The bowl may be held too tightly, especially in tense situations. Any excess pressure applied by the fingers or thumb may tilt the bowl against the bias and cause it to 'wobble' on delivery (see 'Tips on Grip' page 6).

Grip (cont)

Fingertip grip (diagram B3)

This is an extension of the claw grip. The bowls sits near the end of the fingers and creates a larger gap between the palm of the hand and the bowl than the claw grip.

Advantages

Provides maximum 'touch' on fast outdoor or indoor greens. The thumb can also be used to 'sight' the selected line of delivery.

Disadvantages

Unsuitable for heavy greens or wet conditions.

cradle grip

B1)

Bowl is held in the palm of the hand, the thumb around centre.

claw grip

B2)

Bowl is held forward on the fingers leaving a gap between the bowl and palm of the hand.

fingertip grip

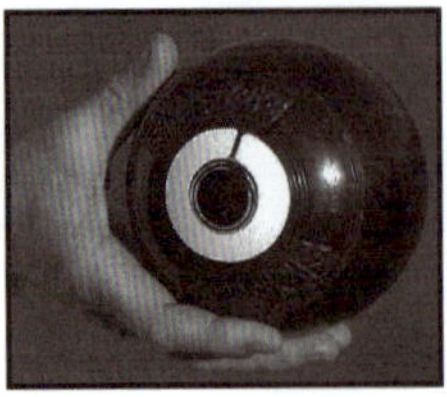

B3)

Here, the thumb has moved to the top of the bowl which now rests on the fingertips. The gap between bowl and palm has increased.

B4)

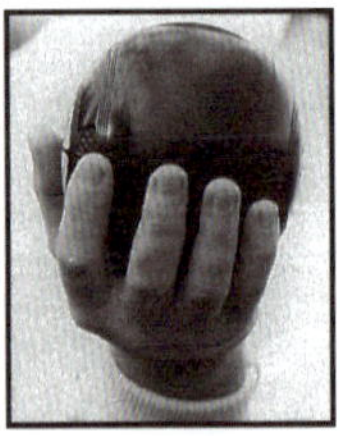

B4 Underside view of the cradle grip. **If the little finger strays round the side of the bowl this could cause a 'wobble' on delivery.**

Grip (cont)

Gripping the Jack

Delivering the jack is an aspect of the game which is much neglected in practice sessions. Having won the advantage of delivering the jack it is important that it can be delivered accurately especially from an extreme forward mat position. As the jack has no bias the delivery line is straight from mat to a point along the vertical centre line of the rink. **The feet should not be angled but run parallel to the centre line.**

Opinions vary amongst players as to how the jack should be held. On the one hand supporters of the palm grip (B5) argue that no spin will be imparted as the jack rolls off the fingers and so it should not deviate from the straight line.

B5)

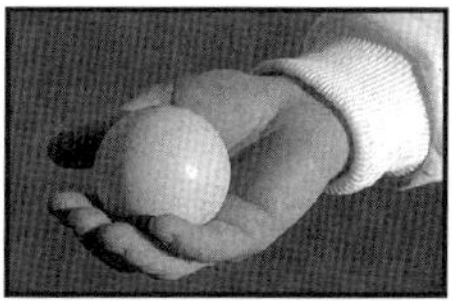

B6)

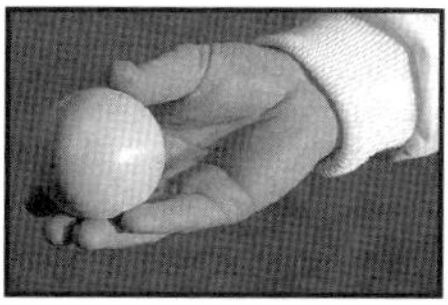

However, this is true only if the wrist remains totally straight during the backward and forward pendulum swing of the arm. The wrist has a natural tendency to turn inwards during the backswing (see later chapter on arm movement) and as the jack is much smaller than the bowl it has more scope to go 'off line'.

With the fingertip grip (B6) where the thumb is on top of the jack, sideways movement of the wrist and forearm is more limited and so there is less chance of deviating from the straight line. For more on jack delivery see page 42.

Whichever method you choose make sure you deliver the jack with the same care as you would your bowl. Possession of the jack is a great advantage not to be taken lightly.

Tips on Grip (forehand)

The following advice should help ensure that the bowl is held exactly in line with its running surface and so is delivered cleanly and without 'wobble'.

a) Balance the bowl on the playing hand as if preparing for a forehand delivery. Do not use the thumb to steady the bowl at this point (diagram B7).

B7)

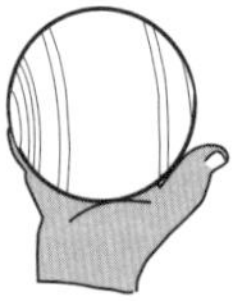

B8)

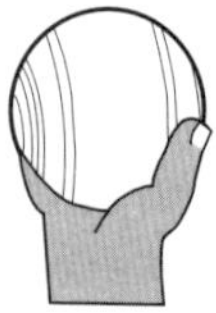

b) Place the thumb on the bowl when the bowl is balanced (diagram B8)

c) Make sure that the hand and forearm are in a straight line. An imaginary extension of this line on the green will be your selected delivery line. (diagram B12 - p7)

You may notice that the grips of the bowl seem to point slightly inwards at an angle to the line of aim (diagram B9). This is the natural effect of the bias. **Any attempt at tilting the bowl so that the grips run parallel to the line of aim (diagram B10) will affect the natural balance of the bowl and create a 'wobble' on delivery.**

B9)

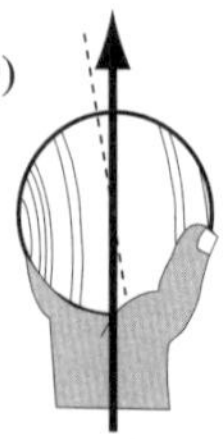

Line of aim ↑ (forehand)

Direction of tilt caused by the bias

B10)

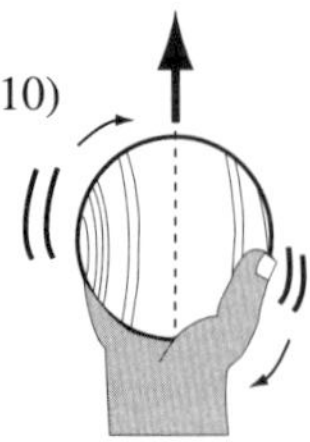

Tilted against bias will cause 'wobble'

Tips on Grip (backhand)

Use the same method to achieve the backhand grip as the forehand.

The centre of gravity of a bowl is slightly off centre and weighted towards the small disc (the bias). When playing the backhand, the line of aim and the dotted line (which represents the angle of tilt towards the bias) will almost be aligned. (diagram B11). This may be one reason why some players find it easier to find the correct line of delivery on the backhand draw.

Backhand position
(right handed player)

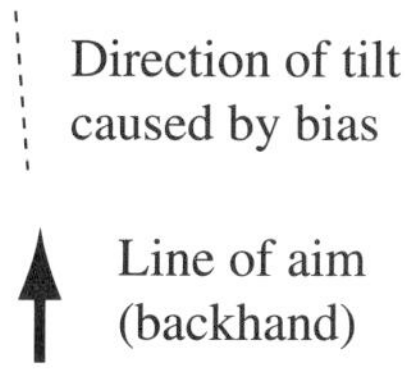

B11)

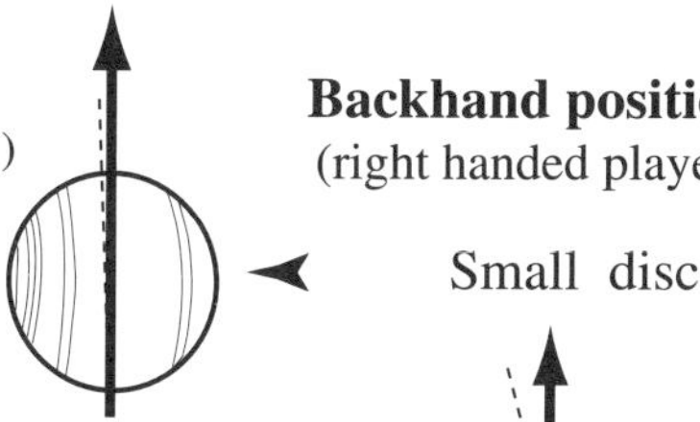

B12)

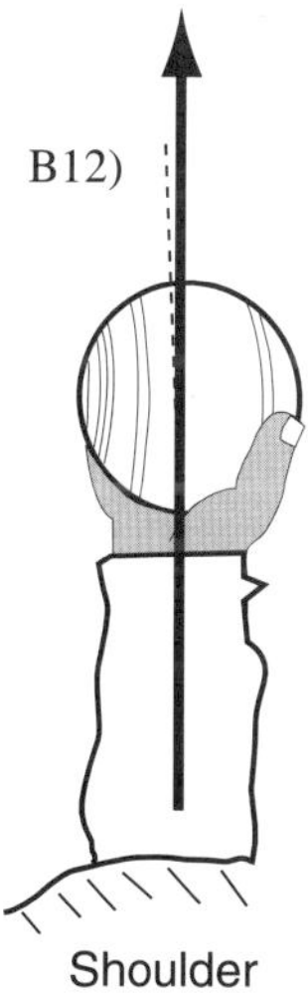

Diagram B12) shows perfect alignment of bowl, hand, wrist and forearm with the delivery line (compare this with B13).

Diagram B13) The player has tilted the bowl slightly against the natural bias which will cause a wobble. The forearm is also at an angle to the line of aim. It is likely from this that the forward swing will come across the body and the bowl will take much more grass on the backhand delivery than was intended.

B13)

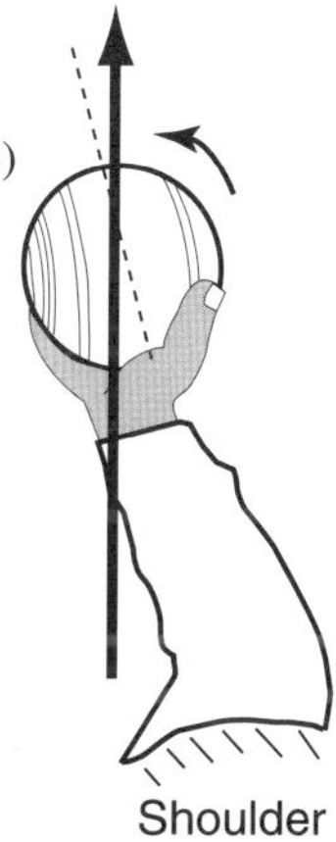

Further Tips on Grip

Another way of arriving at the forehand and backhand grip is demonstrated below. Diagrams B14-16 show how the 'claw' grip can be achieved by right handed players. Left handed players should reverse the instructions for playing and non playing hands.

B14)

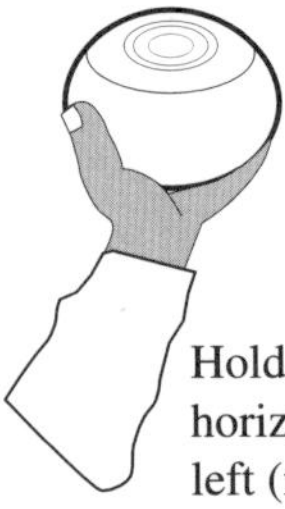

Hold the bowl horizontally in the left (non playing) hand (B14)

B15)

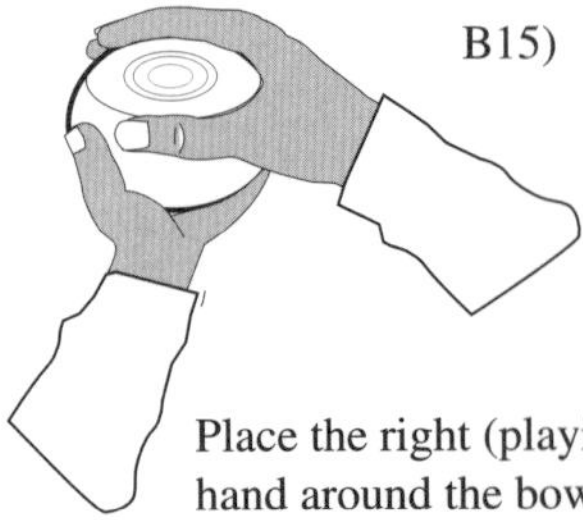

Place the right (playing) hand around the bowl so that the thumb and forefinger are close to or touching the grip (B15).

B16)

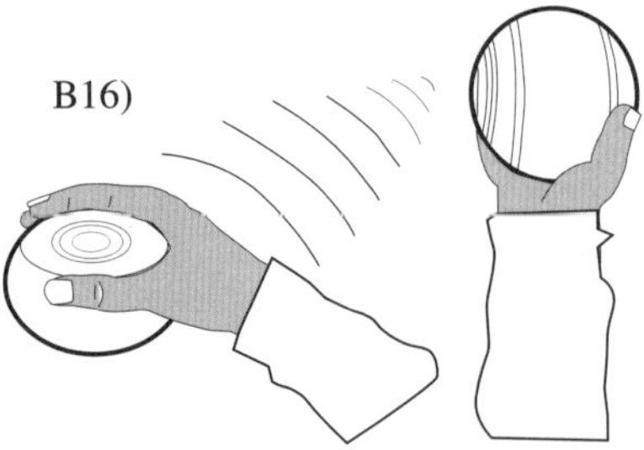

Turn the bowl upright. Check that the hand, wrist and forearm are in alignment (B16).

B17)

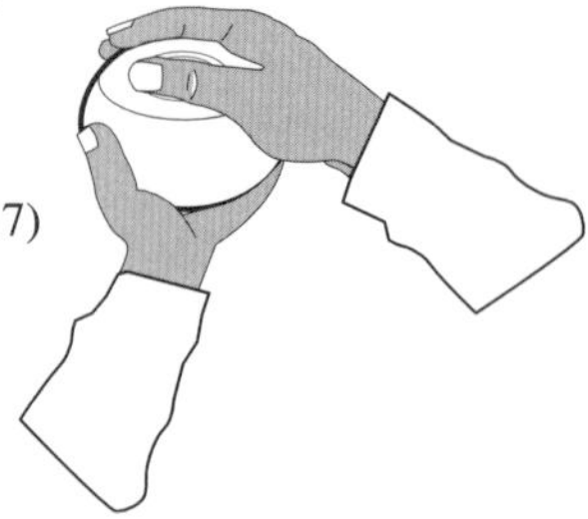

For the cradle grip repeat the exercise with the thumb of the playing hand over or just below the centre disc of the bowl when it is held in the horizontal position (B17).

Delivery Stances

The following positions, show the 4 main stances on the mat: The athletic, semi athletic, full crouch and fixed stance. It is up to the individual which style he adopts but whatever one is chosen must be comfortable and consistent.

C1)

Athletic Stance (diagram C1)
The most natural position from which to deliver the bowl. Knees are slightly bent with the weight on the right foot (right handed player). An all round delivery style which encourages coordination and rhythm. The full backswing possible from this position gives maximum controlled impetus to the bowl without strain - especially useful in heavy conditions.

C2)

Semi Athletic Stance (diagram C2)
Similar to the athletic stance but the back and knees are bent and the bowl is held nearer the green. This style produces a shorter natural backswing - a feature useful for fast running playing surfaces.

Delivery Stances (cont)

C3)

Fixed Stance (diagram C3)
Used mainly in the Southern Hemisphere where the greens are exceptionally fast and little power is required in drawing to the jack. Owing to the limited amount of movement, there is less likelihood of error occurring with this stance. It is not recommended however for normal outdoor conditions found in this country which tend to be much heavier than those in the Southern Hemisphere.

C4)

Full Crouch Stance (diagram C4)
A preliminary position which is adopted before raising the body into a more upright delivery stance (necessary to generate sufficient power for the delivery). Bringing the eyeline closer to the green enables the line to the jack to be assessed more clearly.

Stance - Feet position

One of the reasons that so many bowls do not follow the intended line just after delivery can be traced back to the position which the player takes on the mat. Facing at even a slight angle to the delivery line can cause the arm to come across the body in its forward swing. This would result in a 'tight' bowl being played on the forehand and a wide bowl on the backhand (see page 41).

In photograph D1) a comfortable and natural stance has been adopted for a right-handed player's forehand delivery action. The left foot points along the centre line (1), while the right foot points towards the delivery line (3). On indoor or very fast outdoor greens the direction of the feet and body will be slightly more angled to allow for the wider line, the left foot pointing towards 2 and the right foot at 4. For the backhand delivery the position of the feet is reversed as shown in diagram D2.

D1)

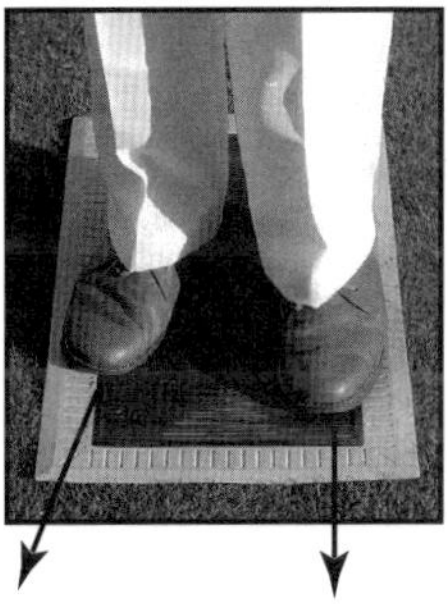

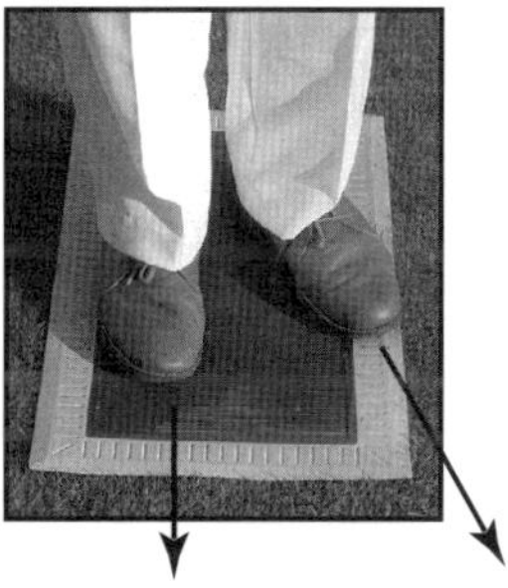

D2)

The trunk of the body should not be twisted but face square to the line of delivery.
This helps to ensure that the arm does not cut across the body on its forward swing.

Feet Position - Using the Mat Width

By using the width of the mat a player can find a new line to the jack which may be necessary in order to go around or inside a short bowl on the delivery line. Diagram D3 shows the normal line taken to the jack by a right handed player.

D3)

Diagram D4 - The backhand line is blocked and a bowl on the forehand is directly on the forehand draw. Standing on the extreme left hand side of the mat with only the right foot on the mat, the player finds a new line and his bowl passes inside the short bowl to reach the jack.

D4)

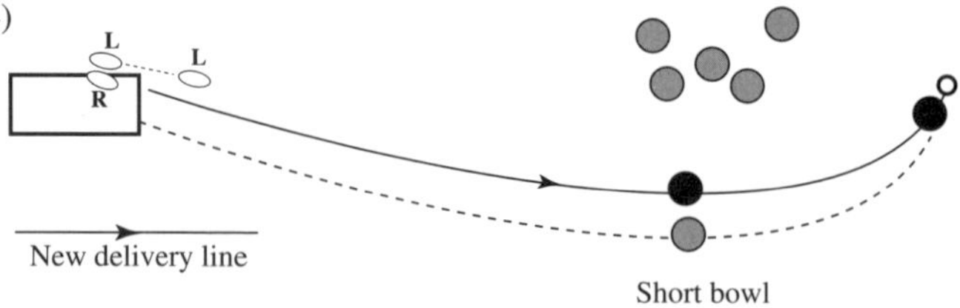

Using the Mat Width (cont.)

A view of the stance taken for an inside line on the forehand (D5). **Check that on stepping out at least one foot is on or over the mat on delivery.**

D5)

The characteristics of the rink may also dictate that a new line be found to the jack. Diagram D6 - The bowl is perfectly weighted but a thin patch of grass on the green causes it to cut sharply across the head and finish to the left of the jack. The inside line is blocked by a short bowl.

D6)

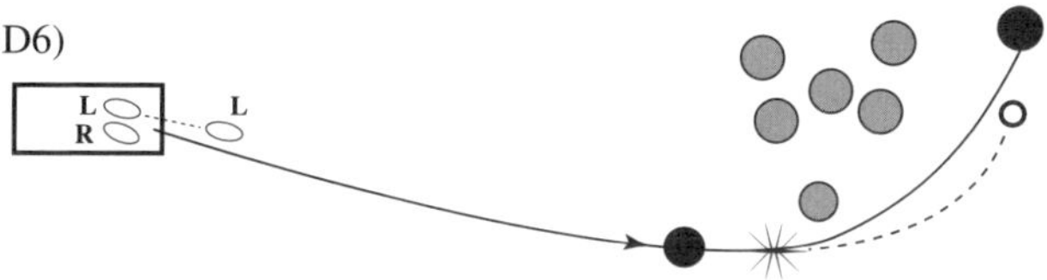

D7)

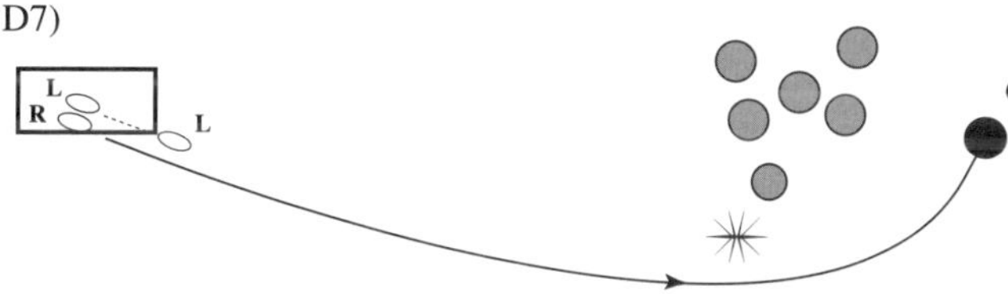

By taking the stance on the extreme edge of the mat as shown in diagram D7, the bowl passes outside the patch of green to reach the jack.

Using the Mat Width (cont.)

The following diagrams show the forehand and backhand positions for **right handed players** to obtain an outside or inside line to the jack. **L** and **R** stand for left and right foot.

D8

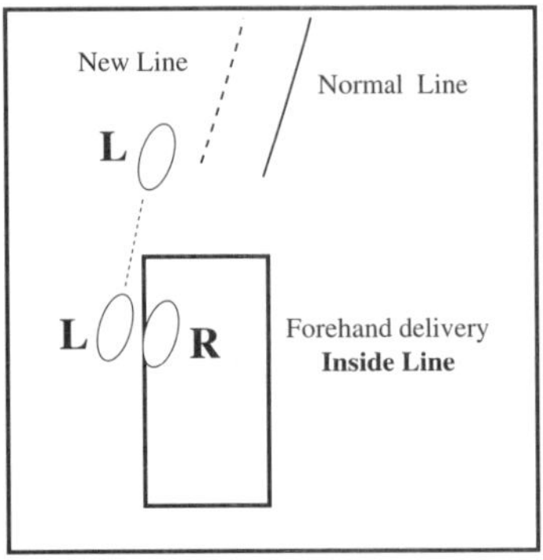

D9

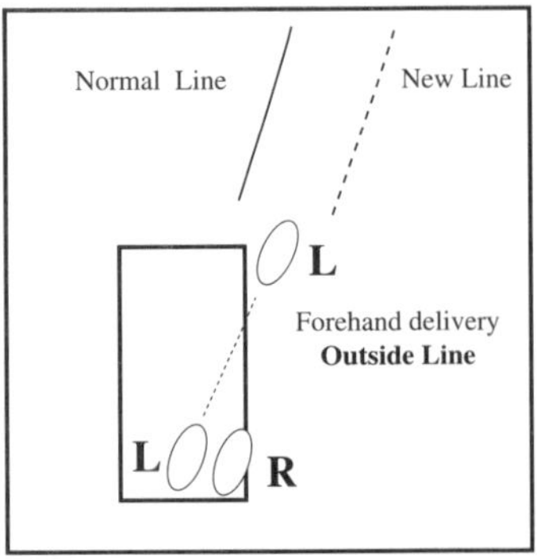

D10

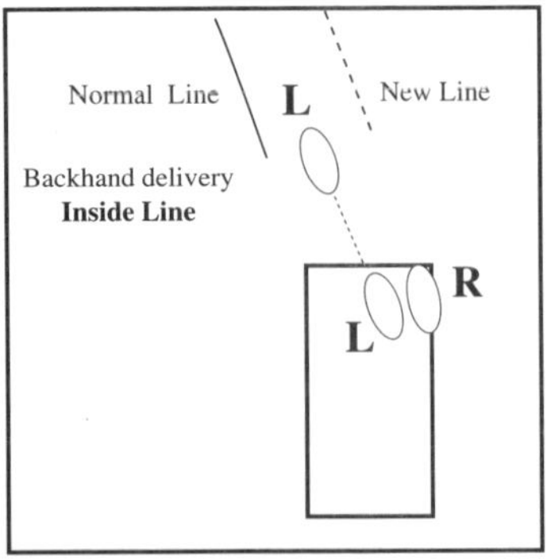

D11

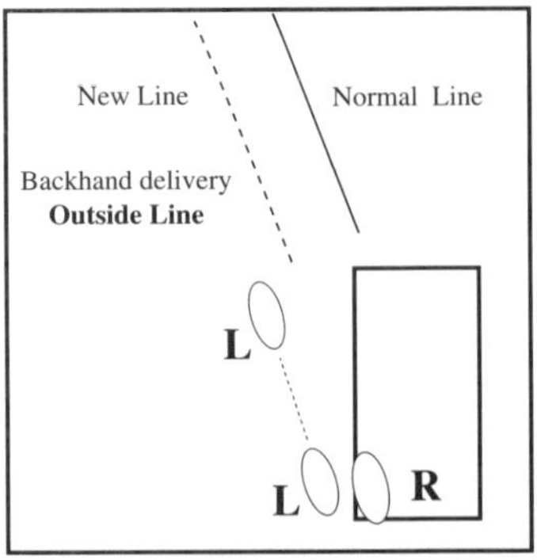

D16

Using the Mat Width (cont.)

Forehand and backhand positions for **left handed players** to obtain an alternative line to the jack. **L and R** stand for left and right foot.

D12

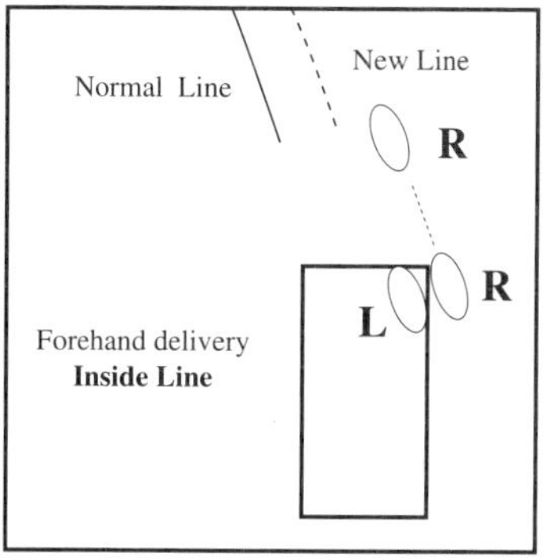

D13

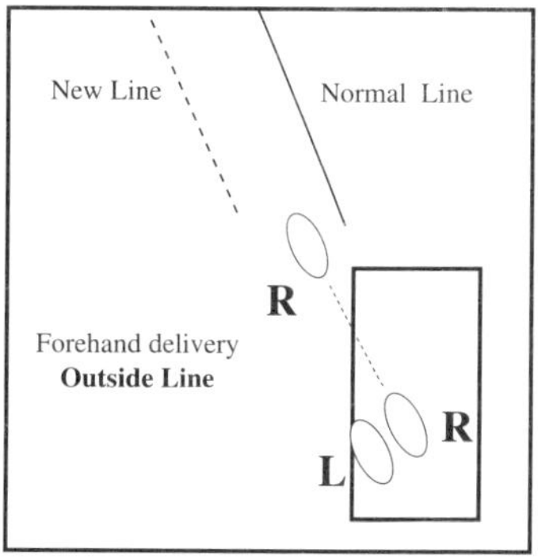

D14

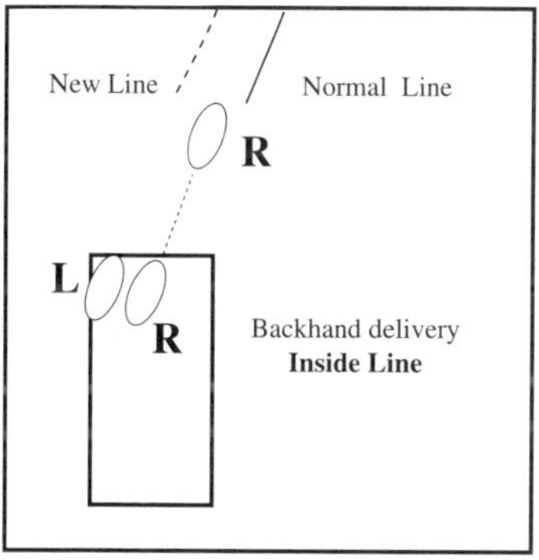

D15

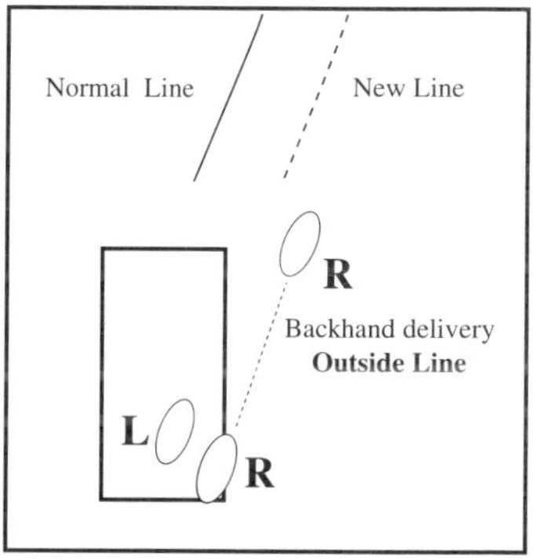

Photograph D16 - The angle of the feet in this photograph indicates that the green is running very fast (body is facing square to the line of delivery). This position was taken to find an inside line on the backhand. The normal line to the jack was blocked by short bowls.

The Swing

The next stage in the delivery, having adopted an appropriate grip and stance is to 'ground' the bowl smoothly on its running surface without a wobble or bounce. Both of these faults are fatal to precise weight and line control and must be eliminated if consistency is to be achieved.

The pendulum swing, combined with a normal step forward which maintains perfect body balance, is the key to a controlled, smooth action whatever stance is adopted (see important note at bottom of page 21).

It is important that the backswing and follow through continue straight along the aiming line. To do this, the bowl, wrist and forearm must be in alignment as described on the previous chapter on 'grip' (diagram B12 - page 7).

The bowling action is a fluid, rhythmic movement. The lead up to delivery can be categorised into 3 distinct headings:

- **Preparation**
  (Checking grip, gearing up mentally for the shot)

- **Stablization**
  (Stance, Balance, Control of nerves!)

- **Concentration**
  (Focusing totally on Line, Length and Pace of Delivery)

There should be a short interval (2-3 seconds) between each stage. The use of a cloth to wipe the bowl during the preparation stage may help to focus concentration and slow down an otherwise hasty delivery.

Swing and Step - Timing

The importance of good timing and coordination between the step forward and the backswing cannot be over emphasised. Without good coordination in this area a delivery will be inconsistent and 'jerky'.

Good timing requires that the foot must not step forward until the arm is well into its backswing and has passed the leg. As the bowl moves into its backswing the knees and trunk of the body bend in time with the backswing ensuring a smooth and controlled rythmic movement. Throughout the whole delivery action the eyes stay focused on a fixed target point. **Any alteration from this point during the delivery could cause the head and shoulders to move resulting in a 'jerk' and loss of line.**

E1
Semi athletic stance: The bowl is held out. Weight is on the right foot and eyes looking along the line of the delivery. The stance should be comfortable and well balanced.

E2
As the arm passes the right leg, the left foot starts its forward step. The heel touches the green first. At this point the body weight is about to move forward.

E3
The left foot is now firmly planted on the green. and the bowl has reached the end of the backswing arc. The body weight has transferred to the left foot.

E4
The body weight moves forward in time with the forward swing. **Notice that the head remains still, eyes focused on the aiming point during the entire delivery action.**

The body should be perfectly balanced when the weight is tranferred from right to left leg (right handed players). An angled swing can throw the body weight sideways with subsequent loss of direction and control.

The Swing - Weight Control

A 'natural' pendulum swing is one of the major factors in attaining good weight control. Fine adjustments on fast greens (varying from several inches to a foot) are made by the middle finger as the bowl leaves the hand.

What is a 'natural' swing?

A natural swing is a term describing the arc of the swing which is unrestricted or unopposed by any force other than that of gravity. In other words a player should not attempt to counteract the natural arc of the bowl in terms of speed or direction. Try the following experiment yourself.

- Place a bowl at the end of your arm (diagram E5)
- Bring the bowl forward to point A (diagram E6)
- Allow the arm to drop **under its own weight**

Its natural backswing brings it to point B.

The further it is brought forward from the vertical the bigger the arc (AA to BB - diagram E7).

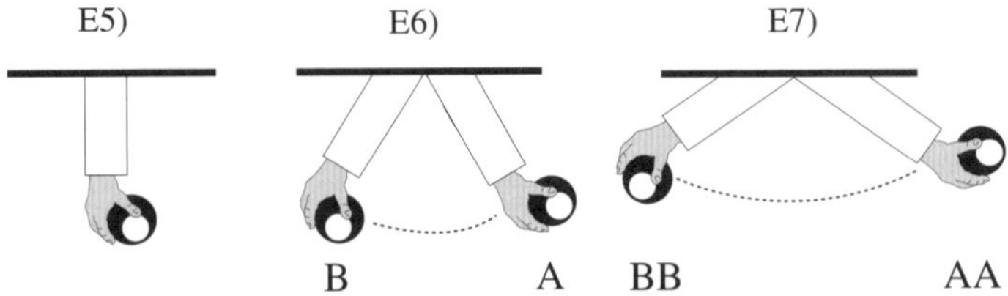

You must allow the bowl to complete its natural backswing. Do not try to swing forward prematurely as this will cause strain and reduce the bowl's speed on delivery.

The Swing - Weight Control (cont)

The length of the backswing's arc in a 'natural' swing is therefore determined by the height above the ground and the distance which the bowl is held from the body in the outstretched arm.

How does this affect weight control?

Imagine a bowl on a narrow chute (diagrams E8-E10). When placed at the top of the chute (E8), it will travel to X.

E8)

Placed near the middle (E9) the bowl will reach point Y

E9)

When placed near the foot (E10) it will reach point Z

E10)

It follows that **all** bowls placed in the positions (E8-E10) on the chute should finish in respective positions X, Y and Z when released.

The 'flick' photographs on pages 1, 17 and 23, further illustrate the positions shown in diagrams E8-E10.

The Swing - Weight Control (cont)

The principles shown in the arm, chute and bowl examples can be applied to the smooth pendulum swing of the bowling action.

It is important that there should be no 'jerk' in the delivery. This fault can be more obvious when playing to a **full length jack** on a heavy green. In diagram E11 the player uses a short backswing to reach a full length jack and is about two yards short.

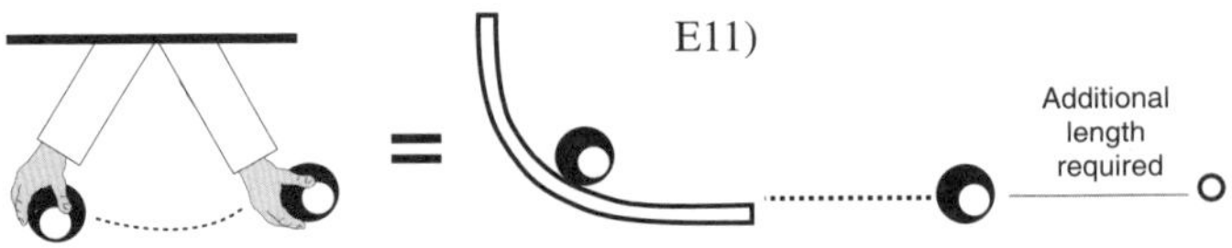

To achieve the additional length he tries to force the bowl forward (before it completes its backswing) - creating tension in the arm, a jerking action and subsequent loss of power and control.

Now, consider the alternative: (diagram E12)
By taking a longer backswing the additional length can be achieved without strain whilst maintaining full control

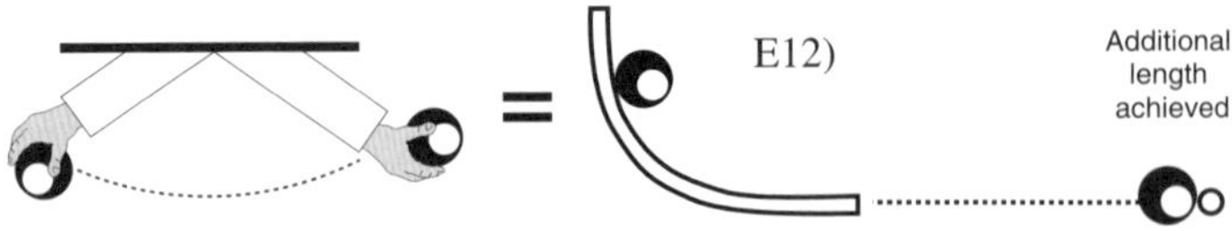

Remember:
Attempting to force the bowl forward before it has completed its natural backswing will also result in a 'jerk' and loss of power and control.

The Swing - Arm Movement

'Weighing the bowl'

You may have noticed some of the top players gently raise and lower the bowl in the hand prior to the backswing. The purpose of this action is to get the 'feel' of the weight required for the shot and also to assist in producing a natural backswing. This method of 'weighing' the bowl (diagram E13) can help those players who otherwise 'pull the forearm down' into the backswing to develop a more controlled and rhythmic delivery. *

E13

* The phrase 'pull the forearm down' describes the action of forcing the bowl into a backswing rather than allowing it to descend under its own weight and speed. This can cause tension in the arm which in turn affects the natural rhythm.

Another claim for this preliminary action is that it also helps with the timing and coordination of the backswing and the forward step.

Important Note:
If you adopt the 'chute' and 'natural swing' principle then the length of step forward should increase or decrease automatically as the body finds its own natural balance.

The Swing - Arm Movement (cont)

It is essential for good line that the swing, no matter how short, is completely straight in its backward and foreward movement. This is not as simple as it seems.

Turning the palm face upwards brings the elbow closer to the body (diagram E14). **If the swing is completely straight then the line of the bowl on its backward arc cannot pass the hip** (diagrams E15, E16).

E14)

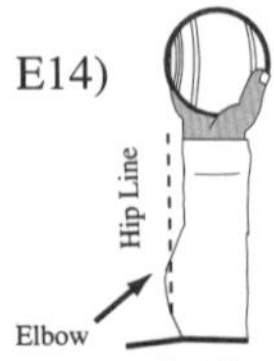

E15)

E16)

E17)

E18)

In diagrams E17 and E18 the weight has been transferred to the right leg and the hip is now 'tucked in'. This allows a) the arm to swing in a straight line and b) the left foot free to take a step forward without first having to transfer weight to the right foot (causing a slight 'sway').

Notice the head position in photograph E17. The eyes are lining up with the bowl and target point on the delivery line like a snooker player lining up his shot between cue ball and object ball.

The Swing - An Alternative Action

Another method of achieving a straight pendulum swing is to allow the wrist to turn inwards naturally during the swing. For a short to medium length jack the hand turns through approximately 90° during the backswing. The action keeps the elbow clear of the hip and again allows the arm to travel freely in a straight line. (diagrams F1-F6). However, this requires perfect timing as the bowl must be straight in the hand when grounded. Consistency will depend on the hand turning through the same angle every time. This is more difficult to achieve with a longer backswing where the hand can turn through 180° .

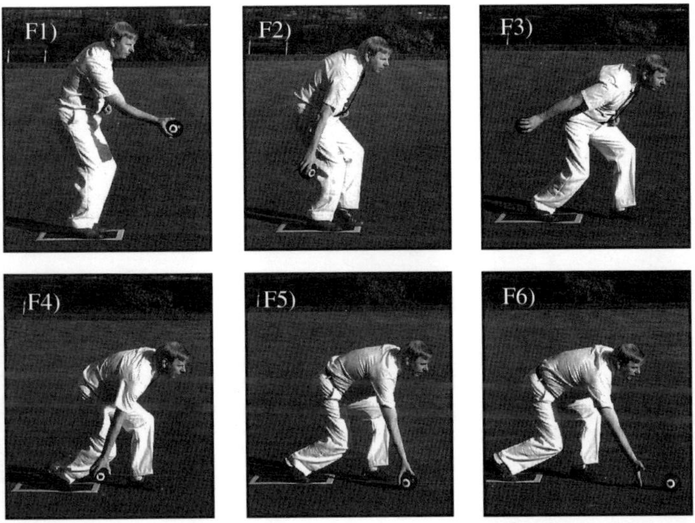

Diagrams F1 - F3 (Backswing)
The hand turns inwards through an angle of approximately 90 degrees.

Diagrams F4 - F6 (Forward swing)
The hand turns back through the same angle and the palm is facing upwards on release of the bowl as in a conventional delivery.

Putting it together - Coordination

So far we have looked at each part of the delivery action separately rather like photographic frames in a reel of film.

Grip, stance, swing, step forward and follow through are all parts of the whole picture - links which require a smooth flow from one element to another .

Photographs G1-G6 show the delivery action where all the elements are blended together. The smooth transitional movement from backswing to follow through takes approximately 3 seconds. Pay particular attention to the timing of the forward step in relation to the backswing.

For a moving demonstration of the upright delivery action (right handed player) flick through the pages of this booklet from left to right. For the semi upright delivery action (left handed player) flick through the pages from right to left.

G1)

G2)

G3)

Delivery action - An analysis

The following checklist is a summary of the stages in a complete delivery action. Left handed players should reverse information where the left and right foot are mentioned.

- Feet position - body facing line of aim.
- Shoulder, forearm and bowl are in alignment.
- Body weight is on the right foot
- Head remains still, eyes looking at aiming point.
- Swing is natural and perfectly straight.
- Weight transfers smoothly from right to left foot.
- Follow through is natural and unrestricted.
- Body stays down after the bowl has been delivered avoiding the possibility of a jerky follow through (G7).

G4)

G5)

G6)

G7)

Eyes are focused on the aiming point and the head stays down until the bowl is well up the green. The body is well balanced throughout the entire action.

Green Speed

The next section in the booklet lists the variety of shots you might be expected to play in a game of bowls. As reference is made to the speed of the green, the terms, slow, medium and fast should be explained in more detail.

Green speed is calculated by the number of seconds it takes a bowl to **draw from the mat** to a standard 30 yard jack.

On a slow green, the bowl will have to be delivered with more power initially, before slowing down quickly as it approaches the jack. The bowl will take less time to reach the jack because of the greater speed of delivery. In the U.K. a green running between 8-12 seconds would be regarded as slow while a medium speed would be around 13-15 seconds.

On a fast green less effort will be required to draw to the jack but the bowl will take longer to stop as there is less green resistance. A fast green in the U.K. is timed between 16-18+ seconds. In the Southern hemisphere where there is more sunshine, green speeds in Summer average around 20 seconds. **The speed of the green will determine the path the bowl will take on drawing to the jack. (diagram H1).**

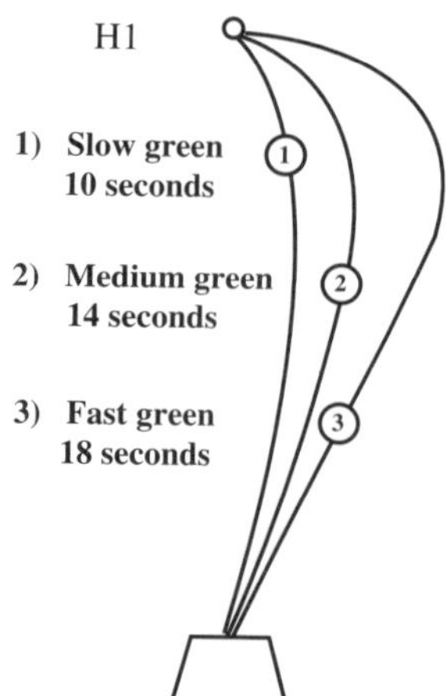

The Draw Shot

The draw shot is the cornerstone of the game of bowls from which all other types of shot arise. The target may be the jack, another bowl or a selected spot on the green for position. Without a complete understanding of this shot and skill in its execution you will be unable to apply modifications to weight and line using the draw shot as the standard reference.

The Delivery Line

The 'Line' can be defined as the path taken by the bowl from the time it leaves the hand till it reaches the jack or selected target. Let us assume that the target is the jack which is positioned at a point along the centre of the rink.

The greater the momentum applied to the bowl the less effect the bias will have. On the early part of its journey to the jack, the bowl travels almost straight in the direction of aim. As it begins to slow down the bias has more influence and 'pulls' the bowl sideways. The path which the bowl takes is therefore an irregular curve (diagram I1).

I1

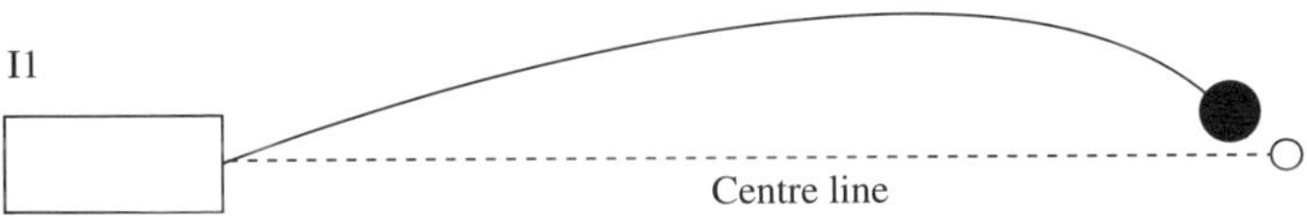

The widest point on the curve is known as the shoulder of the arc **(*)** (diagram I2)

I2

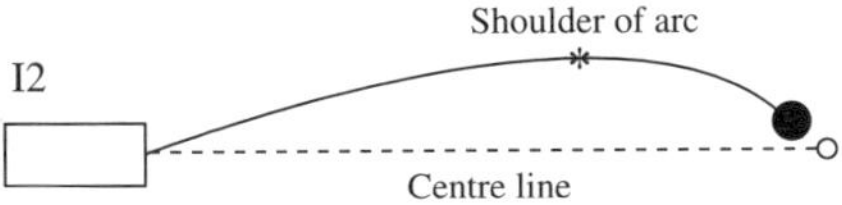

The Draw Shot (cont)

The position of the shoulder will vary depending on the speed of the green. On a slow green (about 10 seconds) the shoulder (*) will be nearer to the mat and centre line than on a fast green. (diagram I3).

1. - slow green
2. - medium
3. - fast

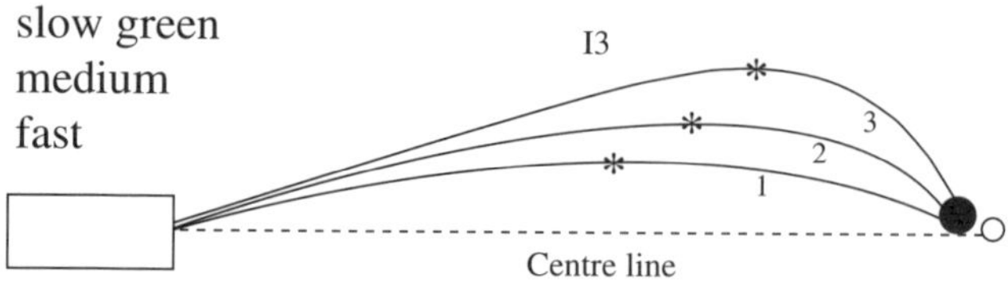

Finding the line

Now, visualise a line (---) from the mat which traces the initial path of the bowl just after delivery to a point on the bank. (diagram I4). This will be your line of delivery. Select a target along this line as your imaginary aiming point. This could be on the bank, or on the green. Personally, I find it easier to concentrate on a point on the line adjacent to the shoulder of the arc (point x diagram I4) **as this keeps any head (and shoulder) movement to a minimum.**

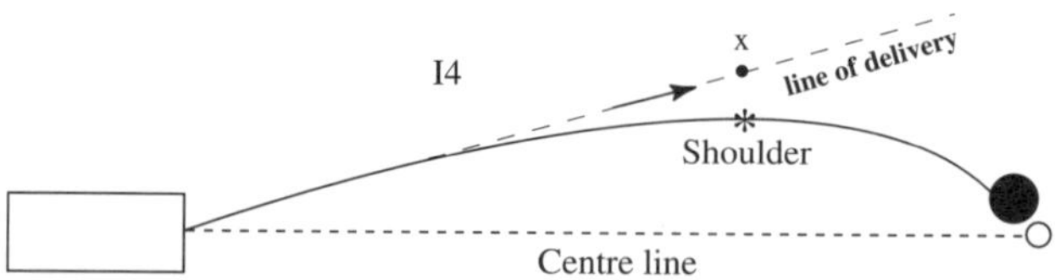

If you were to aim at the actual shoulder then the bowl would be insufficiently grassed and cut across the centre line.

The Draw Shot (cont)

For the purposes of clarity call the point on the line adjacent to the shoulder of the arc (•), the 'imaginary' shoulder.

If the green is running true and the bowl has been delivered cleanly then every bowl following this line should finish on the centre of the rink whether the jack is minimum distance or full length.

Diagram I5 shows the difference in the delivery lines when there is a narrower draw on the forehand than the backhand.

I5

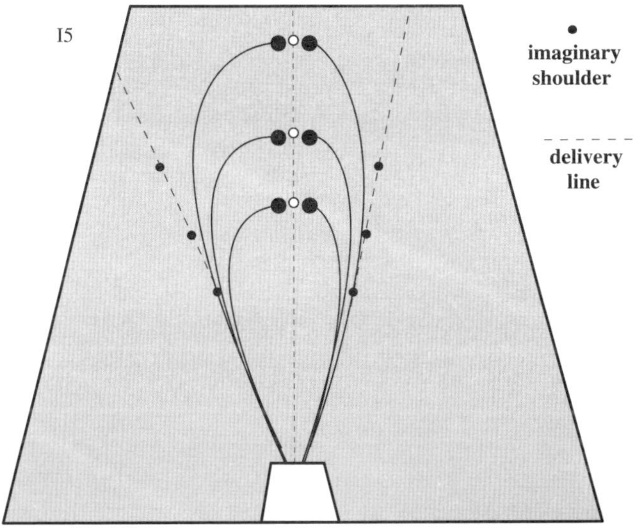

The Positional Bowl

This is a tactical bowl drawn to a specific point on the green such as a 'blocker' (a bowl deliberately placed on a point on a delivery path to protect a player's position) or a covering bowl. If this point is off centre then a new delivery line has to be found. Allowance may have to be made in weight for heavier grass outwith the normal playing track of the rink.

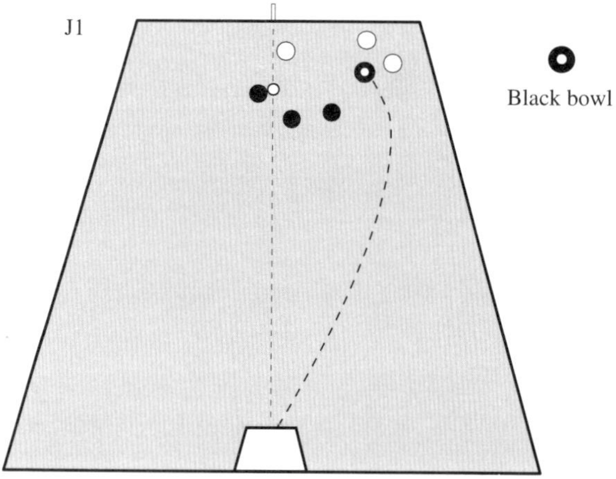

In diagram J1 black holds three shots with one bowl from each player to come. White has the last bowl. Black would be well advised to place his final bowl around position x as any contact on the shot bowl would spring the jack towards white's three bowls (diagram J2)

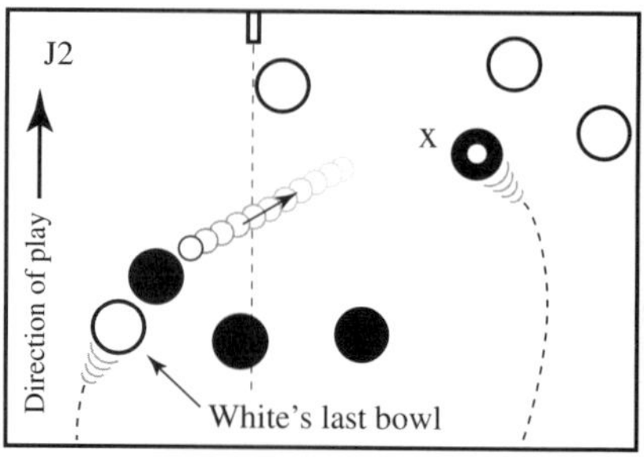

The Chap and Lie

The chap and lie (or tap and lie) is a draw shot played with slightly more pace to enable your bowl to dislodge another and take its place. The target is usually an opponent's bowl but could also be your own when you are trying to improve your position at the head. This is a shot requiring precision especially on fast greens where the bowl takes a wider path to the jack.

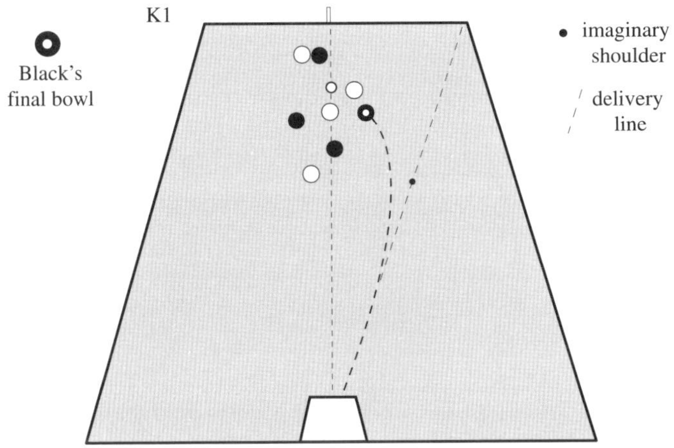

Diagram K1 - white holds two shots. Black has the last bowl to play. Diagram K2 - Black chaps and lies against white's bowl, replacing it for shot.

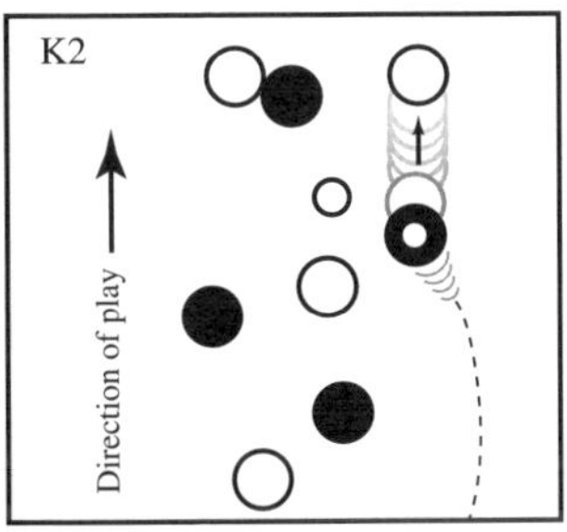

The Running Bowl

The object of the running bowl is to disturb bowls in the head in order to improve your position. Similar to the chap and lie shot but played with more weight. Remember that because of the greater pace of the bowl, the delivery line's approach to the head will be narrower than for the draw shot although the delivery action remains the same.

Diagram L1 - a white draw is blocked on both hands.

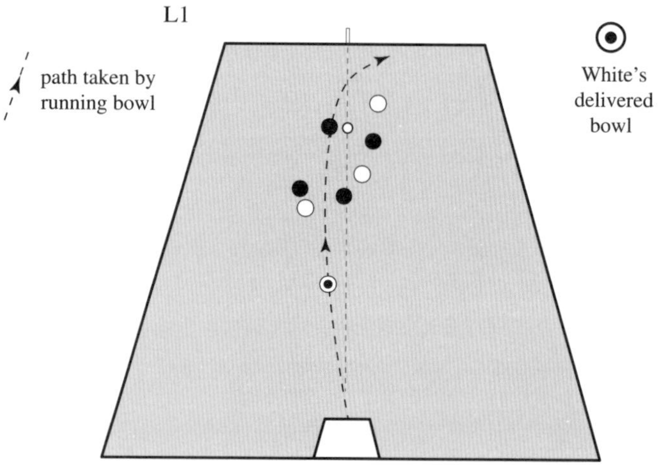

Diagram L2 - White plays a running bowl on the backhand (right handed player) through a narrow gap and moves the black bowl which, in passing, clips the jack towards white's back bowl.

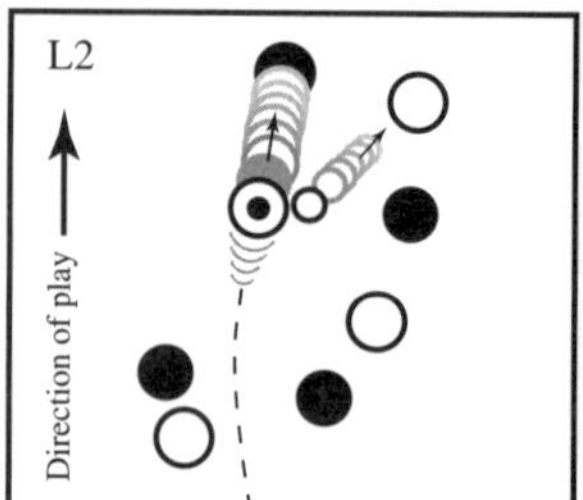

The Wick

The wick shot is where a player aims to hit another bowl at a certain angle so that it then travels in a particular direction like a canon in snooker. Used in a situation where there are few options and the jack cannot be reached directly. Diagram M1 - The score is 20-20 and white lies game. Black has the last bowl. There is no clear road to draw to the jack on either hand and white's blocker prevents a drive. The wick is usually considered to be a lucky shot, and often is, but it is a legitimate shot to play.

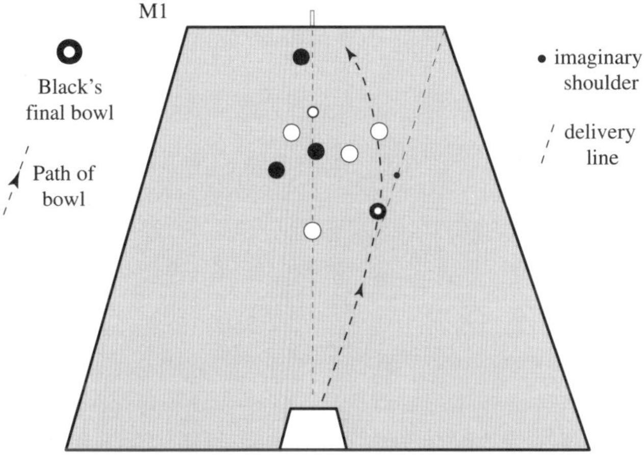

Diagram M2 - black's bowl deflects off white's outside bowl for a count of 1 shot and the match. Slightly more than drawing weight is required for this shot.

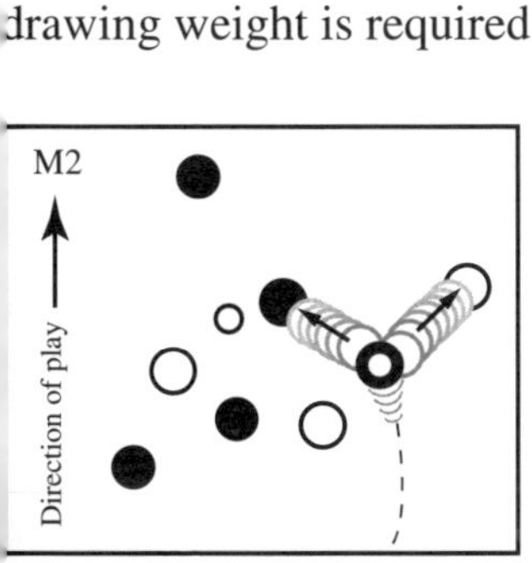

The Plant

The plant is a term used where two bowls are touching or so close together that any contact on the first bowl will send the second in a predictable direction. As the distance between the two bowls increase the direction taken by the second bowl becomes less predictable. Diagram N1 - black lies shot almost jack high. White **could** attempt a draw on the backhand but would have to be accurate within 6 inches of a full length jack to get the shot.

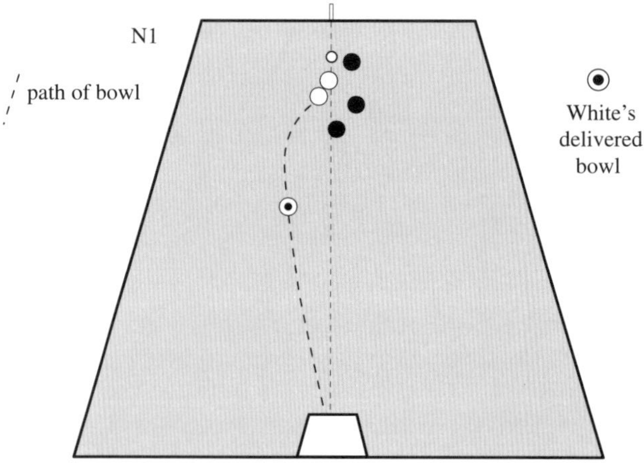

Diagram N2 - White makes contact with the first of his own two bowls with slightly more than drawing weight. The front white bowl in turn contacts the black bowl sending it out the head. White lies 2 shots.

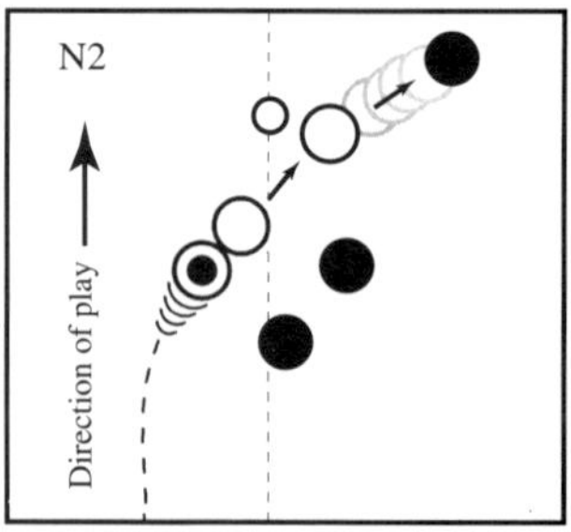

The Jack Trail

Here you are attempting to move the jack to a more favourable position. A difficult shot which becomes even more so the faster the green. Also if you do not make the contact you are hoping for the jack may move towards your opponent's bowls. Diagram O1 - white lies shot and black attempts to trail thc jack to his other three bowls. The delivery line is narrower than for the draw shot.

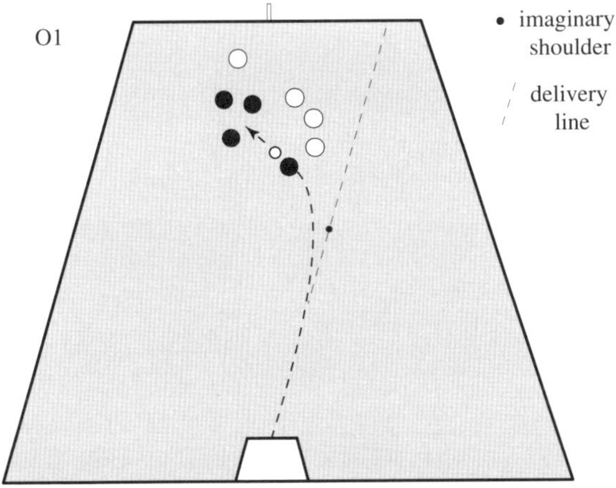

Diagram O2 - black successfully trails the jack about a foot for four shots. However had the bowl been slightly narrower it could have touched the jack on the left hand side slicing it to white's three bowls.

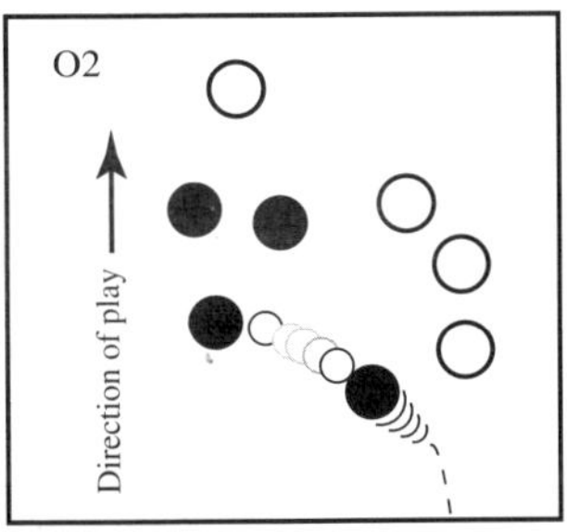

The Drive

The drive is used mainly as a rescue shot when the position is heavily against you and no other shot presents a feasible alternative. Delivered with power, the speed of the bowl should cancel most, if not all of the influence of the bias. On a fast green the delivery line should be straight up the centre line while on a slow green a slight amount of grass may have to be taken. The feet position for this shot should be adjusted as per the delivery of the jack (pages 5 & 42). Diagram P1 - White lies four shots with no touchers.

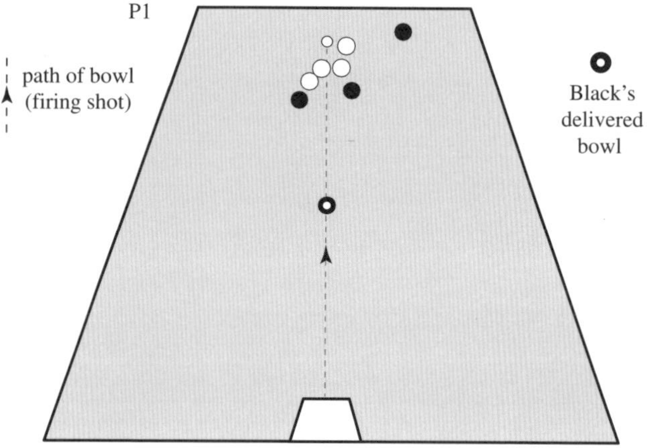

Diagram P2 - Black makes perfect contact with the cluster of white bowls. All of white's bowls go out the rink together with black's delivered bowl. The jack has gone into the ditch (still in play) leaving black counting three shots.

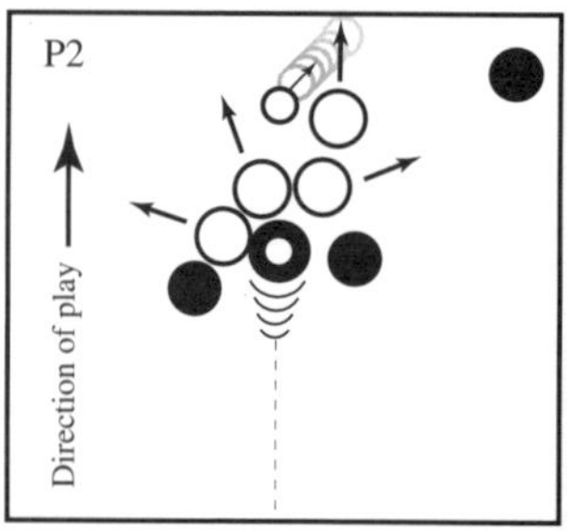

QUESTIONS AND ANSWERS

This part of the manual considers some general and specific questions which have been asked by club members during coaching sessions.

Q I have a claw grip and a semi crouch delivery and find it difficult to play to a full length jack on heavy greens. How do I overcome this?

Increase your length of swing by extending your arm and holding the bowl higher in your stance position. (see pages 18-20). Your step forward should increase in length to maintain body balance and the bowl will travel further without strain or loss of control. Remember not to rush the delivery action and run off the mat.

Q Where should the non delivery arm be on release of the bowl?

Right handed players generally place their non playing arm on their left knee to assist with balance but it a matter of individual preference. The important point is that the non playing arm must contribute to the balance of the body and not restrict the swing or body movement.

Q I have a cradle grip and crouch delivery. Recently (within the last few weeks) my bowl has developed a severe 'wobble' just as it leaves my hand.

A 'wobble' is caused when the bowl is tilted against the bias. It sounds as if your grip has altered slightly and the bowl is lying at an angle in your hand. Read pages 6-8 which describe the problem and how it can be rectified. Bowl 'tilt' can also be caused by the position of the thumb and little finger when gripping the bowl .

QUESTIONS AND ANSWERS (cont)

Q Sometimes when 'I am short' with my first bowl and deliberately give the 2nd bowl 'a bit extra' it is still short Why?

Stopping the arm from completing its natural backwswing will counteract the natural momentum of the bowl and slow it down on its forward swing. If this is the situation in your case 'pushing' the bowl will not necessarily increase the weight. Allow the arm to complete the full backswing.

Q I have an upright stance and find great difficulty in adapting to fast green conditions, especially when playing to a short jack. Why?

This is where players who adopt the semi athletic or crouch stances may have an edge. In these positions the bowl is held nearer to the green when the player is positioned on the mat. The length of the natural backswing arc is reduced and so there is less momentum applied to the bowl on the forward swing. However, a player with a natural upright stance can adapt by:

- *slowing down the speed of the delivery action*
- *bending at the waist and knee more than normal and holding the bowl at approximately knee height, with arm held almost straight - The backswing will be naturally restricted as it starts from a lower point on the 'chute' and the step forward will be shortened (see photograph Q1 and refer to pages 18-21).*

Q1)

QUESTIONS AND ANSWERS (cont)

Q I use the claw grip and believe I have a smooth delivery, but occasionally the bowl 'bumps' the green just before it leaves my hand taking about a metre off the weight. Recently, in an important game, this happened at a crucial time and cost me the match. Why does this happen?

One possible cause of the bowl 'brushing the green' before release is that at one point during the swing there may have been an alteration in the angle at which the bowl approached the green. Bending the wrist at some point during the swing, for example, means that the bowl would contact the green at an angle during the forward swing, rather than running parallel to it. This would cause the bowl to bump into the green before it was ready to be released. (diagrams R1 and R2).

R1)

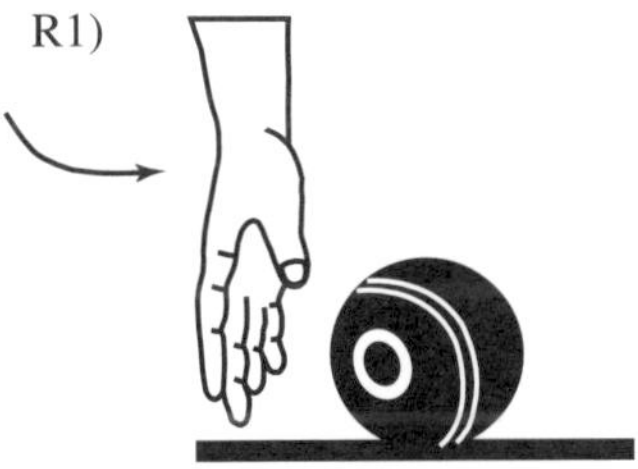

Correct position of hand on release of the bowl

R2)

Bent wrist causes the bowl to approach from an angle and so 'bump' the green

It could also be a lack of concentration, or, if it was at a critical stage in the game, pressure which caused you to tense up the delivery action resulting in bumping the bowl into the green.

QUESTIONS AND ANSWERS (cont)

Q I am guilty of 'bouncing' my bowl on delivery. How do I correct this? I use an upright delivery stance.

One of the causes of bouncing the bowl, (ie releasing the bowl from a height above the green), is the failure to 'bend' the trunk of the body at the waist in coordination with the backswing (photographs S1-S3). Apart from ruining consistency this fault will also damage the green. In photographs S5 the trunk of the body and legs bend in time with the backswing before stepping out (refer also to the flick pictures of the upright delivery action). Loosening up exercises may also help in assisting you to get down to deliver the bowl.

Practice this action until the timing and coordination become natural. It may take time but will be well worth the effort, not only to eliminate the bouncing bowl, but also to develop a smoother and more consistent delivery.

QUESTIONS AND ANSWERS (cont)

Q No matter what line on the forehand I choose to deliver my bowl I always end up playing inside my intended line of aim resulting in a tight bowl. What's going wrong?

It is likely that you are not facing square to the delivery line and/or your arm is coming across your body in the forward swing (usually the result of an angled backswing). Compare the lines taken by the bowls just after release in photographs T1 and T2.

T1)

Body is facing square to the delivery line, eyes focused on aiming point. The arm follows through straight along the delivery line.

direction of delivery line

T2)

The body is facing at an angle to the delivery line and the arm cuts across the body resulting in a 'tight' bowl.

To confirm this is the problem try the following experiment:

- *Stand facing square on in front of a mirror (a full length mirror if possible) and swing your arm as if you were delivering a bowl.*
- *Continue the forward swing until the arm is in a horizontal position with the fingers touching the mirror.*
- *If your arm and its reflection form a straight line then your swing is straight. If the reflection is at an angle to your arm then you are coming across your body when your arm is following through.*

QUESTIONS AND ANSWERS (cont)

Q I have developed a phobia about delivering the jack as when I do it goes everywhere but straight up the rink. I don't understand why this is, as I have no problem finding a line with my bowls or delivering the jack when playing indoors.

There should be no difference in the delivery action between that of a bowl and jack. Assuming your delivery technique is sound, your difficulty could arise from a loss of balance when you are stepping forward. Because it is smaller and lighter, a common fault is to 'throw' the jack rather than 'deliver' it which affects balance (more so on a heavy green). Also, any undue tension caused by your anxiety about delivering the jack will create a jerky action and lack of control. If balance is the problem the following exercises should help.

U1 Hold the jack out with your feet pointing straight up the rink and your **knees and back bent** as in the semi crouch position.

Without stepping out go through the motion of delivering the jack using the pendulum swing but do **not** release the jack. Repeat this action several times.

U2. Now, starting from position U1, take a step forward and deliver the jack about half way up the green. **The length of the swing should reflect the distance the jack has to travel (refer to page 20).**

With each subsequent delivery **gradually** increase the backswing until you can deliver a full length jack confidently and consistently.

QUESTIONS AND ANSWERS (cont)

Q I have a crouch delivery and want to develop a firing shot. I can't seem to give the bowl sufficient momentum to keep a straight line without losing control of direction. I have been asked to skip in a team game and feel at a disadvantage without this shot in my locker.

Try raising the body almost into the upright position from the crouch position as you begin the backswing. This allows greater lattitude for a longer backswing and step forward. Consequently there will be more controlled power behind the shot when your body weight transfers from the right to left foot. Also, you should not try to restrict the forward movement (follow through) of your body as the momentum of the drive may take you several yards up the green. David Bryant, the reknowned professional, adopts a deep crouch position on the mat when drawing but stands upright when he is about to drive.

The following exercise may help improve your accuracy. Place two mats side by side about 1 foot apart half way up the green (diagram V1). Aim to run the bowl through the gap without touching either of the mats. As you become more confident take the mats further up the rink and reduce the distance between them. You should increase the pace of your delivery ***gradually*** *until you find your maximum speed at which you can control the bowl.*

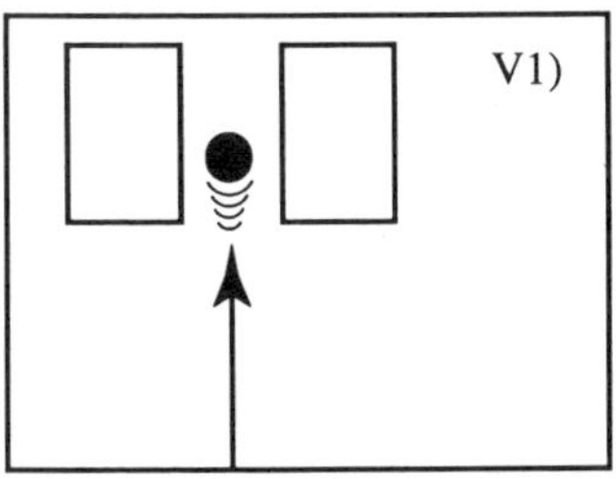

Acknowledgements

I would like to thank the Committee of Management and members of Hamilton Caledonian Bowling Club for their support in the development of this booklet. In particular a special thanks to Tom Wheatley (Club Coach), Lindsay Freeland (Club Coach) and Alan Stewart (Abal Studios) for their assistance with the production.

Most clubs have qualified coaches. Please make use of him/her no matter how small your problem may be.

Alex Struthers
Club Coach
Hamilton Caledonian Bowling Club

And finally..... Some advice for the competitive bowler:

Should you to win at bowls aspire
A sound technique you must acquire
Attend to what is writ herein
If you would learn the way to win.